CUENTO DE LUZ

This collection of children's books, inspired by true stories, comes from the heart. It is the result of a collaboration between the What Really Matters Foundation, and the publishing company Cuento de Luz.

We share the same hopes and dreams, and the same philosophy for promoting universal values.

We hope that families, teachers, and librarians from around the world are moved, inspired, and entertained by these books, and that they discover–if they have not done so already–what really matters.

María Franco
What Really Matters Foundation
www.loquedeverdadimporta.org

Ana Eulate
Cuento de Luz
www.cuentodeluz.com

Emmanuel Kelly: Dream Big!
Text © 2018 María del Carmen Sánchez Pérez
Illustrations © 2018 Zuzanna Celej
This edition © 2018 Cuento de Luz SL
Calle Claveles, 10 | Urb. Monteclaro | Pozuelo de Alarcón | 28223 | Madrid | Spain
www.cuentodeluz.com
Title in Spanish: Emmanuel Kelly
Series: What Really Matters
English translation by Jon Brokenbrow
ISBN: 978-84-16733-40-8
Printed in PRC by Shanghai Chenxi Printing Co., Ltd. September 2018, print number 1649-9

EMMANUEL KELLY

Dream Big!

Mamen Sánchez
and
Zuzanna Celej

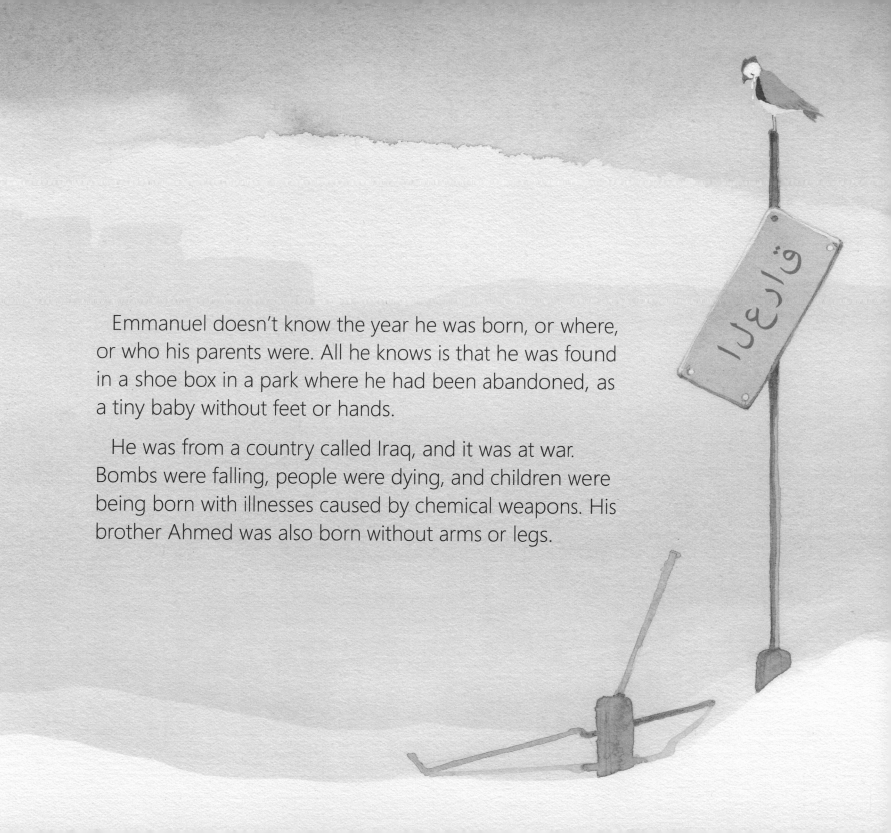

Emmanuel doesn't know the year he was born, or where, or who his parents were. All he knows is that he was found in a shoe box in a park where he had been abandoned, as a tiny baby without feet or hands.

He was from a country called Iraq, and it was at war. Bombs were falling, people were dying, and children were being born with illnesses caused by chemical weapons. His brother Ahmed was also born without arms or legs.

One gray day, when the sun could barely shine through the clouds of sand and dust, two nuns were traveling through the city. In the distance, they heard the sound of a baby crying.

Next to a bush, they found a cardboard box. Inside it was a tiny baby, crying from hunger. It was an angel with broken wings: he had neither hands nor feet. They named him Emmanuel, meaning "God with us", wrapped him in a blanket, and hurried back home with him.

Only a few days earlier, they had found another baby just like Emmanuel, and they had called him Ahmed.

From that day on, the children were brothers. They grew up together in the orphanage where the nuns looked after lots of people with disabilities. Emmanuel and Ahmed, two little boys who were barely able to stand, helped with the chores around the house.

They fed the babies, changed their diapers, and cuddled them at night when they were frightened by the sound of the bombs. The two of them turned out to be the strongest of all the children that lived in the home.

One day, while they were playing in the sand, a beautiful woman appeared. To Emmanuel, she looked just like a fairy with her blonde hair and blue eyes. She told them her name was Moira, and that she came from Australia. "There are doctors there who can cure your little feet," she told them. "It will be like magic: you'll be able to stand and walk."

Ahmed was amazed. Of course he wanted to go to Australia with Moira! But he loved Emmanuel so much, the first thing he thought about was his brother's happiness.

"If you can't help both of us, take Emmanuel first," he said to Moira. "I'll stay here, and wait for you to come back for me."

When she heard this, Moira knew that she had found her sons. From that moment on, she would be their mother for ever and ever.

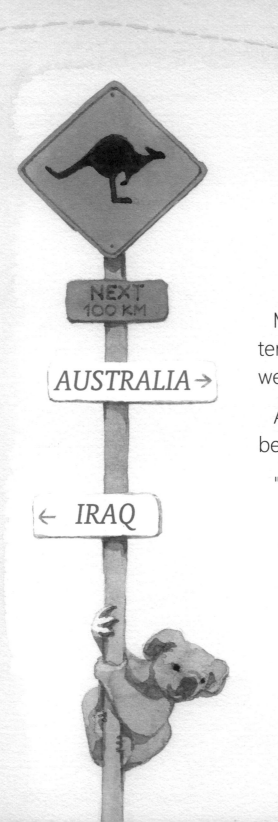

Moira made every effort to save the boys from the terrible war. After a difficult few days, all three of them were finally able to leave on an airplane for Australia.

As they flew through the clouds and saw the world beneath them, they yelled as loud as they could:

"Everything looks so beautiful down there!"

Their new family was waiting for them at the airport. There were so many of them! Uncles, cousins, and friends had all come to welcome the boys to their new home.

When Emmanuel and Ahmed saw the green grass, they rolled and tumbled around in it like two little lambs. Their happiness inspired everyone around them to remember how beautiful the ground beneath our feet can be.

Emmanuel had two operations and after a few months, he was able to stand up and walk, hold on to things, and take care of himself.

Emmanuel longed to go to school. He wanted to learn to read and write. Ahmed bravely played soccer with his new prosthetic legs. He laughed and laughed when he kicked the ball and one of his legs flew off into the air.

The years went by. Emmanuel and Ahmed grew up to be two handsome young Australians. To everyone's amazement, Ahmed decided he wanted to be a professional swimmer. For hours and hours he trained in the sea and the swimming pool, until he learned to swim like a dolphin. When the Paralympic Games were held in London, he swam for Australia.

"It's all about believing in yourself," he said. "You must never give up. You mustn't be afraid of failing. If you feel passionate about something, you must fight for it."

Encouraged by his brother's bravery, Emmanuel decided he wanted to be a singer. Music was his passion, and to make his dream come true, he rehearsed day and night for months.

"There's a path for everyone in this life," he thought, "and it's up to us whether we travel it or not. You have to work as hard as you can, and never be afraid. You have to keep going, however tough things get.

"When he was ready, he entered a singing competition in Australia called "The X Factor," and sang a song that touched everyone's hearts. After his performance, the audience cheered and cheered. Everyone could feel his enthusiasm.

The presenter of the show asked him, "What would you like to do with your life?"

"I'd like to be an inspiration for others," replied Emmanuel. "That when people see me, they think, 'If he can do it, why can't I?'"

"So what advice would you give to a young person who wants to be a success?" said the presenter.

"Dream big!" yelled Emmanuel,

"Dream big!"

Emmanuel's words reached every corner of the planet. There were children who got up off their couches, and began to work hard to make their dreams come true.

Think about it: there's no obstacle or problem that's too big to overcome. If you are ever about to give up, remember that a baby without hands or feet, abandoned in a city destroyed by war, was able to make his dream come true.

If he could, why can't you?

About the *What Really Matters Foundation*

The aim of the What Really Matters Foundation is to promote universal values in society. Its main project consists of the What Really Matters conferences, which are aimed at young people.

Every year, they are held in eight cities in Spain, and in another six countries. During the conferences, a series of speakers share the real and inspiring stories of their lives, which invite us to discover the things that are really important in life, like the story in the book you're holding.

You can join us, hear more stories, and learn more about us at www.loquedeverdadimporta.org.

We look forward to your visit!

María Franco
What Really Matters Foundation